# Doodads
## A Collection of Children's Poetry

Second Edition

by
Carrie Heyes

ISBN: 9781441482563

for Olivia

## Baking Cookies

I was warned that this would happen as I stirred the cookie dough.

"Now, if you eat too much of it, a pain inside will grow."

I didn't really listen as the ingredients swirled around.

I took a nip to try it; a better taste could not be found!

I couldn't stop! I ate and ate... a spoonful here then there.

Before I knew it, most was gone; the bowl was almost bare.

I looked down at my belly. It stuck out beneath my shirt.

And that is when the pain began, the ache - the awful hurt.

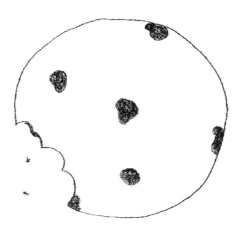

"It hurts!" I clutched my tummy as I sat down on the floor.
"Too much!" I cried to everyone. "The cookie dough... no more!"
I moaned as I regretted having taken every bite.
"I should *not* have eaten *all* that dough! I know now - you were right!"

There was nothing I could do but wait, the ache *would* go away.
I knew it must eventually. It couldn't stay all day.
I sat and waited patiently, and pouted; rubbed my tum.
Then I heard the ding-dong ring... the cookies! They were done!

Well, cookie dough and cookies are two very different things,
For my tummy feels much better once the oven timer rings.
It knows the fix for **too much dough** is cookies. I am sure.
It doesn't really make much sense, but b'lieve me it's the cure!

3

## ... freckles. ...

I've lost my freckles! They're not **on my** face.

**They** disappeared **without warning!** They're gone, **with** no trace!

**What** a disaster. **What** a disgrace!

Oh, **why** can't I keep my freckles in place!

## The Dreaded Words

"First one in bed gets the first tuck-in!"

At those words my heart would pound,
I would not hear another sound.
It's *my* turn to get the first kiss tonight.
First Mom will turn on *my* night-light.
I run up stairs and down the hall,
Only to hear my sister call,

"I'm in bed first!"

So close to bed my heart would sink,
As all my hopes went down the drink.
I'm always last to get tucked in,
But I was *sure* tonight I'd win.
Then as Mom leans near my bed
She whispers,

"You get two kisses instead."

2 Kisses

## 4 Leaf Clover

Nose to the ground, I search to and fro.

I know there's one here

'Cause it's where clovers grow.

I'll look 'til I find one ('course, more would do).

'Cause I want to find out

If their magic is true.

First off, I'll spy one and then mark its spot.

I'll talk to it, feed it

And water it a lot.

My four leaf clover will grow big and tall.

So big, in fact,

That it'll make me feel small.

Just imagine the wishes a big clover will give,

As I love it and feed it

And help it to live.

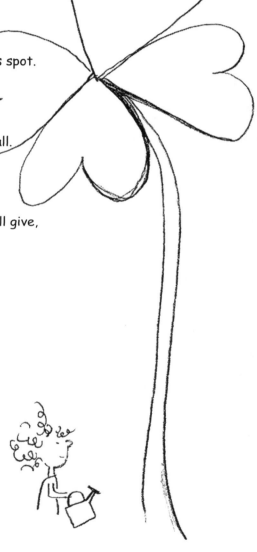

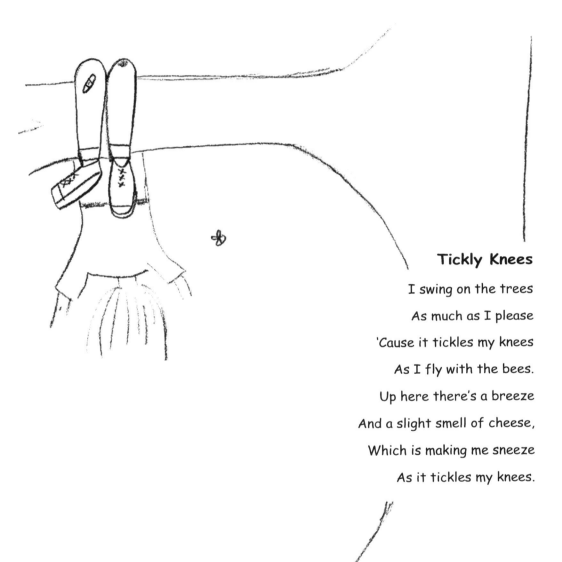

### Tickly Knees

I swing on the trees
As much as I please
'Cause it tickles my knees
As I fly with the bees.
Up here there's a breeze
And a slight smell of cheese,
Which is making me sneeze
As it tickles my knees.

## Jammies-with-Feet

Jammies-with-feet! Jammies-with-feet!

I'll wear nothing else – these cannot be beat!


I can slide on the floor. I want nothing more.

All other jammies are such a big snore!


My toes – they are toasty. My body is roast-y.

I love my jammies-with-feet the most-y!

## Spectacles

I have two special windows, through which I see the world.
The frames of them are pinky-rose and 'round my ears they're curled.

Everything is bright and clear; upon my nose they sit.
I can see things far and near, and they have just the perfect fit.

Not all kids need spectacles that change the way they see,
But my magic eyes are wonderful and they're a part of me.

# Nap Time

My Mother tried to trick me right after I ate lunch.

I got my favourite blanket and a book – okay, a bunch.

Together we began the book.

Well, Mom would read

And I would look.


She thought this made me sleepy, while we snuggled close in bed.

But it's Mom who soon was tired and her eyes drooped as she read.

Eventually the reading stopped.

Mom's eyes had closed,

Her head had flopped.


Luckily I can read myself. I pick up where she left off.

But gosh my bed is cozy and my pillow feels so soft.

I'm done the book. Can't trick a kid!

On second thought...

Maybe sleep I did.

## Mini Whale

I just got a fish tank, but nothin' lives there yet.

First I'll put some water in an' then I'll be all set.

My Mom said, "Get a turtle." My Dad said, "Get a snail."

Both of those are good ideas... but I think I'd like a whale.

Nothing big or fancy - just a little one will do.

I'll feed him mini marshmallows and maybe call him Stu.

He'll like it in my fish tank, swimming to and fro.

He'll come up to the surface, then take a breath and blow.

Stu will be my best friend, an' I'll teach him to play ball.

He'll live with me forever, as long as he stays small.

## Tree House

"Pull up the ladder! Lock the trap door!

We must defend our fortress or it won't be ours no more!"

I can see the people coming through the peephole in the wall.

Luckily they're so far away they still look pretty small.

But wait! They carry weapons! They're ready to attack!

"Put on your helmets everyone, we've got to fight them back!"

They come closer without warning. I hear them holler out.

I do not wait to listen and hear what it's about.

"Duck!" I cry to Allie. "Peter, you must not speak!

Where are they?" I ask Jenny. "Why don't *you* go take a peek?"

Then as we huddle closely, we hear a knock from down below.

We lower down the bucket (but carefully, nice and slow).

We hear rustling and movement but cannot see the ground.

We hold our breath and wait it out, until there's no more sound.

"Pull up the pail!" I order. "We'll explore what's left inside.

We are very strong, brave warriors – no need for us to hide!"

Phew! It's safe, we got supplies. Mom has brought us lunch!

Sandwiches and crackers, juice and grapes - a bunch!

## Visit

I love you, I love you, I love you!

I'm coming to see you soon.

We're leaving to visit you, Grandma,

After lunch at noon!

I miss you, I miss you, I miss you!

I'm going to come and stay,

At your house with you, Grandpa.

I hope you're ready to play!

## 5 Cent Candy

It takes all morning to walk to the candy store.

I creak open the door,

Step onto the floor.

All around me is sweet, wonderful delight.

I try with all my might,

To pick each one just right.

Candy that's chewy or hard, some big and some small.

Tasty treats fill each wall.

I really want to try them all.


I walk up to the counter once, twice, thrice.

I keep checking the price,

(Buying candy's my vice).

I wanna use up my money 'til every cent's gone.

What I spend my money on,

Is each kind of bon-bon.

I leave with a brown bag of goodies. Yum yum.

Soon they'll be in my tum.

Maybe next time you'll come!

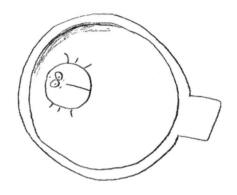

## Captured

Today I found a bug.

Then I put him in a mug.

Now inside it, I will let him be.


He has a lot to eat.

But he has no friends to meet.

Gee whiz... I hope no one does this to me.

## Movin' It

traipsing bouncing flopsing dancing

skipping hopping twirling prancing

## Where I Live

I live on a cloud where it's soft and light.

The sun shines down on me, warm and bright.

I live in a dream where everything's real.

I can alter my world to suit how I feel.

I live in the air and float where I please.

I twirl 'round the stars and dance with the trees.

I live very close in a far away land.

I'll show you, just trust me and lend me your hand.

## Sick

I'm sick... I need a Popsicle to lick.

I'm shivery... my tummy feels all quivery.

I'm hot... I feel way worse than I thought.

I'm sore... I can't stand it anymore.

My head... it feels as heavy as lead.

My nose... hurts every time it blows.

My throat... I need an ice cream float.

I'm sick... this is **not a trick**!

## Dust Bunnies

All day I chased-ed bunnies.  They live all 'round my home.

They're mini, fluffy, tiny puffs. They like to 'splore an' roam.

They like to hide in corners, behind doors, under my bed.

Sometimes they run across the floor, so careful where you tread.


They're sneaky lil' devils as they hide just outta sight.

But I know all the spots to look with my trusty flash-a-light.

I scoop their fluffy bodies up then release them to the breeze.

They'll be happier outside I think - they can live among the trees.

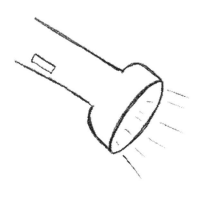

## Both Sides

I like to keep things tidy. Yep. I can't stand a mess.

Otherwise to find my stuff, I can only guess.

I take care of *all* my toys by putting them away.

That way, not a thing gets lost and there's tons of room to play.

I feel *better* when my room is clean, all tidy, nice and neat.

I feel calmer, lighter, happier – a feeling you can't beat!

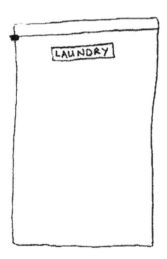

I like to keep things messy. Yep. I don't like them clean.

'Cause if I put my toys away I don't know where I've been.

I forget what I was doing if I tidy all my toys.

It's like only having si-a-lence when all you want is **noise**!

Having all my stuff in sight reminds me what I've got.

Sometimes I want to get new toys then see – I *have* a lot!

To be fair, I see both sides. Either way our lives will bloom.

But living *would* be easier if we didn't share a room!

## Bunk Beds

The top's the best. It's got a ledge.

I lie on my belly an' look over the edge.

I'm king of the hill, from way up here.

I'm not 'fraid a'heights. I've got no fear!

From so high up the view is fine.

I sure am glad the top bunk's mine.


I prefer *my* bunk. It's underneath.

It's much more private. That's my belief.

Just hang up blankets on the side,

It makes a cave in which you can hide.

My bed's a fort, a home, a nook.

If you want to, you can peek in an' look.

## Going, Going, Gone

I went for a walk. I found a rock.

I gave it a swift kick down the block.


I went for a run. My lace came undone.

I tied it up then kept chasing the sun.


I went for a hop. A skip, jump, kerplop.

I ran off the dock and did a big belly flop.


I went for a float. On a big motorboat.

We kept going in circles, all round the moat.


I went for a fly. With the birds in the sky.

I'll be gone once you look, so take care, good-bye!

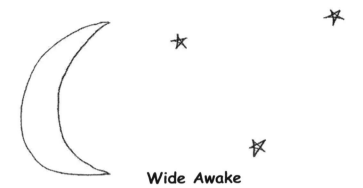

## Wide Awake

I'm not tired. I don't want to go to bed.

I don't feel sleepy, wanna stay with you instead.

I'm not tired. If I sleep I'll miss the fun.

When I wake it will all be over - finished, kaput, done!

I'll go to my bed later, when all the adults do.

I will. I promise. Honestly. Believe me, 'cause it's true!

I'm not tired. I could stay awake 'til dawn.

Really. I'm not fading fast. I'm wide awa... (big yawn).

## Gum Tree

Is it true? Is it true? If you swallow your gum
A long time from now, a tree will grow in your tum?
'Cause I chew it a lot and sometimes it goes down.
Even if it's an accident, will it still stick around?
Will it grow up my throat then stick out my ears?
Please let me know. I'm quite close to tears!

Unless, on the other hand... more gum would sprout.
"Look at the gum factory!" people would shout.
Wrists made of bubblegum, chewy elbows.
I'd have bubbly hair and gumballs for my toes!
How perfect... fantastic! No need to buy -
I'd grow gum all over - an endless supply!

## Birthday Party

I didn't get invited to the birthday party. So?

It doesn't really matter 'cause I didn't wanna go.

It won't be great - I don't like cake, balloons or goodie bags.

I don't want to watch her open presents wrapped with bows and tags.

I'd rather play outside and get my jeans all stained with grass.

Wear a party dress and shiny shoes? No thanks! I think I'll pass.

For my big day, when I turn 6, I've planned a lot of fun!

I'll host my party out-of-doors. There'll be room for everyone!

## Helper

I helped Nana sew a button on, puttin' thread in through the hole.

Then Mommy sent me on a hunt for her wooden salad bowl.

I found it after I zipped the zip on sister's favourite dress.

I was getting pretty busy, but I can handle stress.

Our neighbour borrowed flour, which I had to go and fetch.

Gramps asked me to play ball with him, he'd throw and I would catch.

Dad needed all my muscle to open up a jar,

But it was *really* stuck and so I didn't get that far.

I mean honestly, I was tired! I had run around all day.

Only helping others out, no time for *me* to play.

Finally I'm off to bed; can't help you anymore. My head - it hurts,

My brain is tired, my feet and back are sore.

What *would* you do without me? In our family *I'm* the glue...

Well fine, you guys, I sorta guess that you are helpers too.

## Traffic

Where are they going? Like ants in a row,

Slowly creeping along. To where? I don't know.


So many people, each one in their car...

Off somewhere different, maybe near, maybe far.

What are they thinking? As they drive by...

Are they loud, are they quiet? Friendly or shy?


Everyone's going. They're all on their way.

But which ones are coming? Who's going to stay?

**peep**

peep. peep. p-peep peep peep. p-peep peep peep peep peep peep

cheep!

## My Afternoon

If I lie still, I feel each blade. Grass moving, it crinkles beneath.

I stretch out my arms and point my toes. My finger tips brush a leaf.

The wind begins to blow a breeze, hair tickles across my face.

The clouds are moving quickly now. They're in a floating race.

The big cloud shifts, the light's so bright! I have to shut my eyes.

I feel the warmth all over me as sunlight fills the skies.

## Thank You

One day I got a jellybean from old man Fred.

"Ooh. What do you say?" Mom asked, nodding her head.

I looked at the bean in my hand. It was red.

Then I looked up. "I want twosomes," I said.

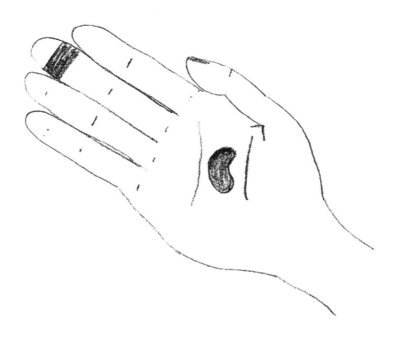

## Into the Water

Run and jump

Plug your nose

Try a jack-knife

Touch your toes

Belly flop

Canon ball

Or dive right in

I do them all

## The Dead Give-Away

How does she know? She always can tell

what was for breakfast. And lunch - that as well.

Teachers are sneaky... there must be a way

that she knows what I've eaten for two meals that day.

All it takes is one look, "Yes, you're right ma'am.

I had toast, peanut butter and strawberry jam.

And for lunch, my favourite. Mmm, mac n' cheese.

How did you know? Will you please tell me? *Please?*"

She winked and then passed me a clean nap-a-kin.

"One day you'll find out," she said with a grin.

## The Future

I'm going to the future so I can live among the stars, fly around in spaceships (up there we don't use cars).

So much waits to be explored, can't let it go to waste. I'll soar right through our solar system, into outer space!

I'll leave the Milky Way and fly to galaxies galore. I'll see a super nova; find a star and search its core.

I'll blast past different planets, drink hot chocolate on the moon, disappear inside a big black hole, race time – I'll fly past noon!

Then I'll ride an asteroid as it shoots across the sky.  Don't you also want to know 'bout what it's like to fly?

I'll spend my time with aliens, learning how they talk... and eat and live - what games they play. It's really gonna rock!

I'll discover something magical that no one else has known. Maybe then I'll leave the future an' decide to come back home.

BOK

Hi

hei

## French or Mandarin?

I'm learning a new language and it's stretching out my brain.

Translating makes me tired so sometimes I have to strain.

Each sentence is not equal; words are not the same.

Trying to figure it all out is sorta like a game.

How do I say? or What's that word? That sounded all a-jumble!

I try so hard to pronounce each word, an' enunciate, not mumble.

Was that the word for cup or grass or Friday... or just a name?

It's hard to keep them straight because they sound so much the same!

Don't talk too fast! I can't keep up... sometimes I get discouraged.

But then I 'member, I learned English. Then I find the courage.

'Cause learning stuff is always hard. Keep trying and stick to it.

You'll make mistakes but that's okay 'cause I know you can do it!

xin chào

hola

nihao!

ciào

sat sri akal

Bonjour

szia!

JAMBO

## Twirling Trouble

I'm in a smidge of trouble 'cause I twirled a piece of hair.

It spun around my finger and it twisted up to there.

Usually this is how it goes. I twirl right to the top.

But today I kept on going! My finger wouldn't stop!

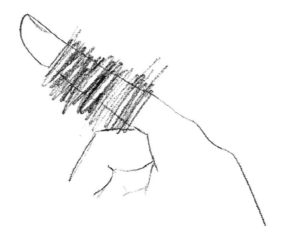

My finger's stuck! It won't come out. It's starting to turn blue...

Unfortunately, there's only one thing I can do.

We're going to have to cut it out - I'll have a big bald patch!

My Grandpa thinks it's funny, 'cause our hair-a-dos will match.

Too bad... I liked to twist and twirl the hairs upon my head.

But had known that this would happen, I'd have twisted yours instead.

## Silly

"Is silly bad?

Some people get mad

when I'm silly. They say that it's dumb."

"No. Silly's not bad,

my dear little lad.

Those people? Their sillies are numb."

## feeling badly

Yeah. I want attention... that's why I'm being bad.

I'm lonely. And I feel left out. My feelings hurt. I'm sad.

## Smelly Markers

One yellow lemon plus a very mint-y green,

Strawberry red and a blue one that smells clean.

A grape-smelling purple and a cotton-candy pink.

Plus a brown one that smells like... chocolate, I think.


What did I draw? A very colourful moustache!

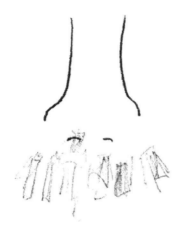

## Aunts

I have a pair of funny aunts who love to sing and love to dance.

Allyn and Kathy are their names and oh, we play such silly games!

I know their songs all off-by-heart. We sing them in the super mart.

We three laugh all through the day, when we sing and dance and play.

So if you ever get the chance, pick up some aunts who sing and dance.

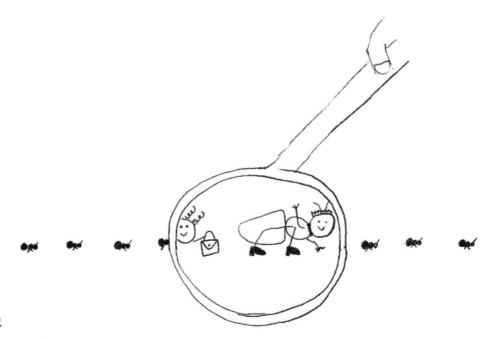

# Swamp Water

(a recipe)

Orange juice with Coke, then add a dash of Sprite.

(Stir it slowly with a twisty straw to make it taste just right).

Some cherry juice and cherries add a lot more fun.

Then say the magic words and your drink will be all done:

*Apouff ofmagic duz thatrick! Thiswamp wadder wownt make-u sic!*

## The Peanut Jar

I know where peanuts come from 'cause I found them by myself,

One day when I got an orange off the kitchen shelf.

Mom cut my orange into boats; I took a whopping bite.

But there was something strange inside my mouth that didn't feel quite

right.

Out I spat a peanut! And then another two.

By the time I ate my orange I had spit out quite a few.

Seven peanuts from my orange sat upon my plate.

The choice was mine to then decide: what would be their fate?

Daddy munches peanuts, especially in the car.

And so I took them off my plate and put them in the jar.

Just for Daddy.

## Dark

There is no scary Boogie Man, or so says my friend Lou.

There's no monster in my closet to jump out and holler, "Boo!"

There's nothing to be frightened of, in the dark of night.

But still I think that (to be safe) I'll turn on my night-light,

(and keep the door open too).

## Bare Legs

I hate nylons. I refuse to wear them.

They cling, they itch,

They make me twitch

And I always seem to tear them.

The crotch hangs low,

They squish my toe

And I simply cannot bear them.

## Sparkles in the Sky

They're very cool, these sparkly stars.

Not seen from cities or from cars.

    They only pop out

    When I'm out and about,

        Camping with my Dad.


He sees lots of things at night,

Pictures in the bright starlight.

    He sees chocolate bars,

    Like my favourite, Mars.

        And it makes me glad.


Maybe Dad can't see too well,

Perhaps it's hard for me to tell.

    'Cause when he sees Mars

    I just see stars,

        But gosh I love my Dad.

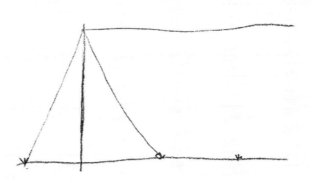

## The Order of Things

Get dirty before a bath.

Play before you clean up.

In case you get too full, eat your dessert before your sup.


And at bedtime (*sigh*): pee, flush, wash and brush.

## Patient Me

All day I have been waiting,

As patient as can be.

I dare not move, I'm in a groove,

Sitting oh-so-quiet-ly.


Since I have been waiting,

My hair has grown a mile.

A puddle dried up, my dog had a pup

And I still have to wait a while.


The paint is dry, a turtle passed,

I learned to dance a jig.

But if I am my patient self

I know one day I'll be big.

## Names

If there's

Plain Jane, Slow Joe, Chatty Cathy, Crabby Abbey, Slim Jim and Even

Steven...

What's Sylvia?

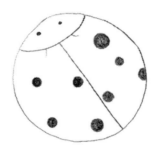

## Miss. Bug

Lady Bug, oh Lady Bug!

Nestled there inside my rug,

You must feel so warm and snug!

If you were bigger, I'd give you a hug.

## The Morning Fight

I have pretty hair. Everyone tells me so.

But why I have to brush it, I will never know.

Each morning I do argue, before to school I go,

That I don't need to fix it - just stick in a bow.

My Mom says that "it's tatty" and then I scream out, "No!"


And so she cut it all right off and will not let it grow!

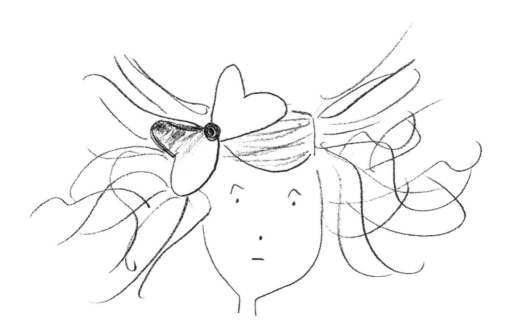

## I'm Innocent

I'm not a scallywag or a little rag-a-muffin.

I didn't pull off Teddy's ear and take out all his stuffin'.

I'm not a troublemaker or a nosey tattletale.

I didn't *make* Eliz'beth eat the cat food that was stale.

I'm not a whippersnapper or a rascal (*all* the time).

I'm just bein' a little kid. Is that really such a crime?

## Bed Wrinkles

I am three, but I'm wrinkle-y,

As crinkled as I'll ever be.

I was in my bed, resting my head,

"Too tired to get up!" I said.

There I lay and there I would stay...

But then Jill called me over to play.

So up I sat, but my skin wasn't flat.

I looked sorta like a giggle-ma-tat.

"From lying in bed," that's what Jill said.

"Next time the wrinkles will be *in* your head."

And so now I know to **get up and go!**

'Cause I don't want wrinkles – at least 'til I grow.

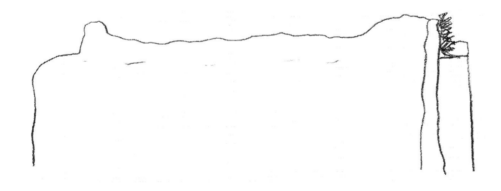

## The End

*The end* means that it's finished. It's over and it's through.
Whatever it was, it's all done now. There's nothing more to do.
But it's not sad, don't worry. Yes, it's true, *that* part is done.
But it also means something's starting, a beginning's just begun.
While one thing is wrapping up, something new is on the rise.
So buckle up, get ready. What's next? It's a surprise!

# INDEX

Made in the USA
Charleston, SC
13 April 2010

4982005R0